150 Best Terrace and Balcony Ideas

150 Best Terrace and Balcony Ideas

HARPER
DESIGN
An Imprint of HarperCollinsPublishers

First published in 2013 by:
Harper Design
An Imprint of HarperCollins*Publishers*
10 East 53rd Street
New York, NY 10022
Tel.: (212) 207-7000
Fax: (212) 207-7654
harperdesign@harpercollins.com
www.harpercollins.com

Distributed throughout the world by:
HarperCollins*Publishers*
10 East 53rdStreet
New York, NY 10022
Fax: (212) 207-7654

Editorial coordinator: Claudia Martínez Alonso
Assistant to editorial coordination: Ana Marques
Editor and text: Irene Alegre
Art director: Mireia Casanovas Soley
Design and layout coordination: Claudia Martínez Alonso
Layout: Cristina Simó Perales
Assistant to layout: Kseniya Palvinskaya, Paco Ortiz García
Cover layout: Emma Termes Parera

ISBN: 978-0-06-221028-9

Library of Congress Control Number: 2012951243

Printed in China
First printing, 2013

CONTENTS

Introduction

From time immemorial, outdoor spaces have been essential parts of a house. Three hundred years ago, the most privileged spent much of their free time strolling through the gardens on their property, and they gave high priority to enjoying the outdoors as a way to improve health.

Today, most homes have outdoor spaces that their owners can use for the activities they find most agreeable and interesting, including barbecues, enjoying a pool or a hot tub, sunbathing, eating, or playing and chatting late into the night. The inhabitants of houses decorate and fit out outdoor areas to meet their particular needs. It is also increasingly common in large cities for skyscrapers to be topped by spectacular roof gardens or adorned with balconies that can be used to escape and forget the hustle and bustle of the metropolis and that add greenery to a gray horizon.

Few spaces in a home are more usable and rewarding than those that allow us to enjoy the outdoors, especially if the temperature is pleasant. It was for this reason that we decided to prepare a book on terraces, patios, and balconies, to take inspiration from the latest trends and learn to apply them to our own outdoor spaces by tailoring them to our preferences and means.

Terraces

This curious house, located on the edge of Lake Austin, has an original circular structure that is complemented by the undulating hills, thus highlighting the landscape that surrounds it. The curve of the staircase emphasizes the geometrical shape of the house even more. The house blends in with the area and becomes another feature of the landscape.

Architect: Bercy Chen Studio
Location: Lake Austin, TX, USA
Photography: Paul Bardagjy

001

In the large outdoor areas, shadows create spaces that can be used throughout the day, depending on the time and the intensity of the sunlight.

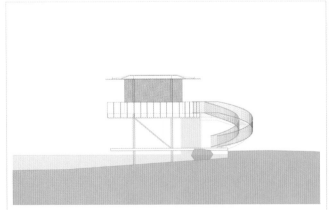

East elevation

002

The waterfall creates a link
between the house and the lake.

003

In this oval space, the seating follows the contour of the large window. The backs of the chairs, the armchair, the center table, and the fan emphasize the elliptical shape of the viewing point.

Casa en Playa Palabritas

The house was designed to create a frame for the view of the beach and the islands in front of it. The aesthetic of the house celebrates the summer, with modern curves that call to mind the Brazilian architecture of the 1960s. The house has a white finish with color accents in red. The dining and living rooms are placed so they can be integrated with the terrace by simply sliding the glass doors.

Architect: Metrópolis
Location: Lima, Peru
Photography: Elsa Ramírez

004

One side is decorated with a concrete lattice that allows light to enter without forgoing privacy.

005

The edges and rounded forms that dominate the whole house soften the geometric and cubic lines of its architectural structure. The various components bring coherence and unity.

006

The bedrooms have access to this interior patio, which is simple and spectacular in the bareness of its forms and decorations.

Abo House

This house derives from an outdated original residence with small windows and an unattractive façade, which meant it needed remodeling. Large windows that can be opened and closed were added, and the overly long hallway that led to the bedrooms was removed. The local climate is very hot, especially during the summer, so they placed smart windows that can control the amount of light that enters the house.

Architect: Nico van der Meulen
Location: Louis Trichardt,
South Africa
Photography: David Ross

007

The house is surrounded by water features that help humidify the air in the hottest months.

Floor plan

008

The outdoor furniture
is combined with the
furniture inside the house
to create a sense of unity
and consistency in which
stridency has no place.

The pool is located between two spaces: indoor and outdoor.

Leaf House

Architect: Mareines + Patalano
Arquitetura
Location: Angra dos Reis,
Rio de Janeiro, Brazil
Photography: Mareines +
Patalano Arquitetura

The roof of this house in Brazil is the main focus of its architectural structure, and it is this feature that provides it with a practical, self-sufficient cooling system. There are no corridors between the rooms, and social areas are sited in semi-open zones. The varying ceiling heights create breezes to counteract the humid and extremely hot local climate.

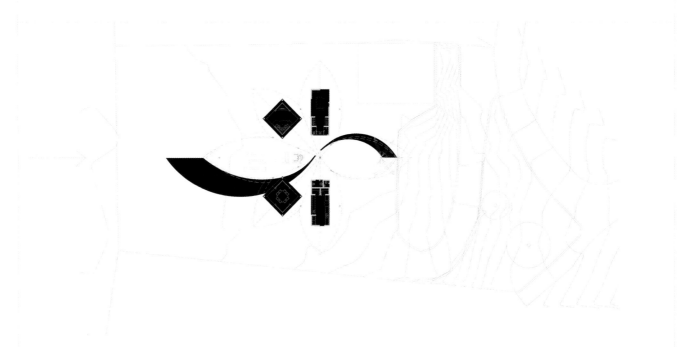

Site plan

009

The roof imitates the petals of a flower and is inspired by Brazil's Indian architecture. It protects the house from excessive sunlight while allowing light in sideways to illuminate the rooms.

010

Palm trees need sun and need to be surrounded by vegetation. Their damaged leaves and branches require pruning from time to time, and they have to be repotted every two or three years.

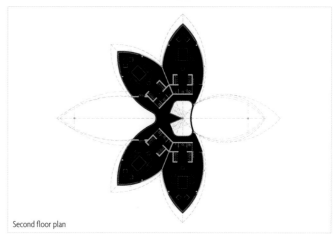

Second floor plan

011

On the terrace, a curious curvilinear pool enters the house. The pool also snakes down to a jetty leading out into a lake.

012

Hammocks are very commonly used in hot climates and are ideal for taking a good afternoon nap outdoors. They are also easy to put up and are economical and lend a tropical feel to a terrace.

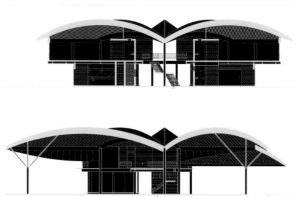

Sections

Landscape design: Roberto Silva
Landscapes (Roberto Silva)
Location: London,
United Kingdom
Photography: Roberto Silva

This small, romantic courtyard is divided into two areas. On thin wooden decking, a white table with a matching parasol presides over the space closest to the house. Across the yard, potted flowers gracefully decorate the entrance to a small studio. A wrought-iron bench that has been painted white adds a touch of nostalgia.

013

The creepers that tumble down the walls simply and effectively beautify the patio. Make sure that the ivy grows in a shady spot, as it does not do well in excessive light.

014

Ceramic pots are porous, which makes moisture levels easier to control. Also, they do not get as hot as plastic pots.

015

The wrought-iron shelf and bench go well together, and the white flowers help the combination of the two colors to work.

This house, designed for a large family, meets the needs of its residents in its 2,874 sq. ft. (267 m²). A number of levels were created on the terrace by using timber platforms, steps, and built-in seats. A striking water feature stands next to the entrance in the front garden. There are several playful aspects to the space, including a plant passageway designed for children's car racing.

Landscape design: Secret Gardens of Sydney
Location: Sydney, Australia
Photography: Peter Brennan

016

The toys are tough and resistant to rain. The blue and red colors match the cushions on the bench and are not out of place in spite of their proliferation.

017

The spectacular water feature at the entrance adds elegance to the space, and its simple white lines relax visitors and do not overly decorate.

Randwick II

This terrace with pool is located in the middle of the city. Ornamental pears and jasmine take center stage in this space. The family that lives in the house makes full use of the space, which has a pool, barbecue, and herb garden. The side entrance is a wall of green bamboo, which provides a beautiful view from the living areas of the house.

Landscape design: Secret Gardens of Sydney
Location: Sydney, Australia
Photography: Jason Busch

018

Despite the greenery, the most prominent color in this space is turquoise. This is due to the great blue mass of the pool bottom, which is emphasized by the prints on the cushions.

019

The combination of pots on this shelf may seem arbitrary, but a close look shows that the balance of tones and sizes is broken only by the different textures.

Contemporary Bauhaus on the Carmel

This house imitates the Bauhaus style, which had its heyday in Israel in the 1950s, twenty years after it began in Germany. The Bauhaus style is characterized by simplicity in its lines, uniformity in color, and spatial continuity, attaching importance to light and ventilation. The roof hovers over the building, consolidating the various parts of the structure.

Architect and design: Pitsou Kedem Architect (Pitsou Kedem, Irene Goldberg, and Hagar Tzvi)
Location: Haifa, Israel
Photography: Amit Geron

020

The bonsai's curves give the space an Oriental air and contrast with the pool, the glass walls, and the house's structure of simple, geometric lines.

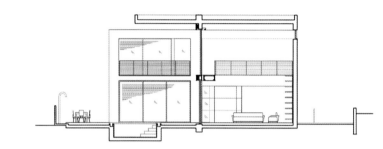

B-B section

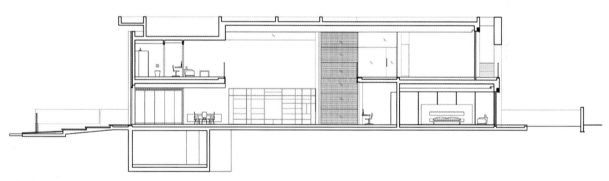

A-A section

Eos

Architect: Víctor Cañas
Location: Faro Escondido,
Costa Rica
Photography: Sergio
Pucci, Francesco Bracci,
and Víctor Cañas

Eos stands near the sea but behind other buildings, so a design was used to make the most of this situation. The main areas and a terrace with a pool were placed on the third floor so they were at the height of the sea. The result is an almost complete union between the two spaces where the horizon of the terrace meets the sea.

021

The terrace stretches across the entire floor, which means that all the rooms have access to the pool. This achieves a first-floor effect and affords immediate access to the outdoor spaces.

The glass balustrade performs its
function without spoiling the views.

022

This corridor has aluminum latticework and is always open, which serves to connect the rooms and ventilate the entire house. The decor turns it into an indoor-outdoor space.

023

The terrace at the height of the sea gives a feeling of space and circumvents the other buildings surrounding the plot.

This house has been refurbished and expanded to accommodate a large family. Changes included adding a new garage, a library, a pool, and a playroom, which was made by converting the old garage. Stairs were added to connect the old spaces with the new ones. Its stone exterior, columns, and the pool, which borders a steep rock face, give the ensemble the grandeur of a villa.

Wiston Gardens

Architect: Luigi Rosselli
Location: Sydney, Australia
Photography: Justin Alexander

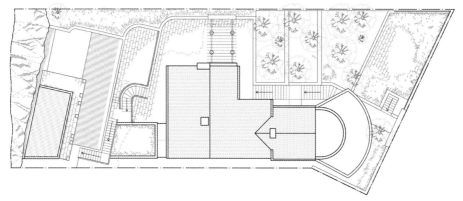

Alterations and additions site plan

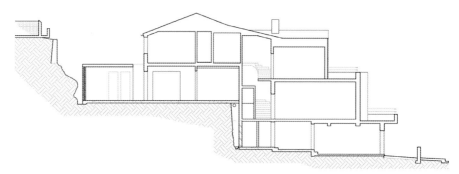

Alterations and additions section

024

This inner courtyard links
the two floors, and the plants
turn it into a garden. Its light
colors make it look bigger
and help illuminate the interior
of the house.

025

The porch next to the pool calls to mind ancient classical buildings, but its columns have a very contemporary shape. In contrast, the columns of the inner courtyard are rounded.

This residential complex situated a hundred yards from the colonial church of Santa María Ahuacatlan has nine town houses and several shared amenities, including a pool and hot tub area that is the central core. The project was designed to adapt to the site and its surroundings, taking as inspiration the other buildings in the neighborhood and complying with the local authority's strict regulations. The houses are divided into volumes sited in an L shape.

Architect: Hierve Diseñería
Location: Valle de Bravo, Mexico
Photography: Alejandro Villarreal

026

The spaces are separated by great arches with thick columns that bring sobriety and simplicity to the complex. In the background, a row of sun loungers with red mattresses continues the geometry of space.

027

Stone is one of the key elements in this construction, and this space, decorated with stones piled in a corner, reminiscent of a dam, demonstrates this detail.

Maison Bioclimatique

This house was built using organic architectural principles and green energy components. The result was maximum efficiency using the minimum of technical elements. It is sited in an area with an oceanic climate, so a garden was designed to protect the house from the westerly winds, and a separate vegetable garden was created on the east side. The roof is clad with 12 in. (300 mm) of Rockwool insulation.

Architect: Patrice Bideau
Location: Brittany, France
Photography: Armel Istin

028

An arbor connects the kitchen to the terrace and is a winter garden in cold weather. The roof is made of polycarbonate.

029

The wrought iron of the table and chairs takes second place to the beauty and originality of the colorful mosaics that cover them. These can be made by hand and at home.

030

The bottom of the natural pools is gravel or clay, and aquatic plants are used to clean the water instead of chemicals.

Casa 6

The design of this house is laid out around the veranda, which in the tropical climate of Brazil is a very commonly used space, where the interior and exterior come together. The veranda in this house is perpendicular to the lounge and covers a living room with a TV and part of the kitchen, which continues in the interior of the house. A studio was added in back. The doors separating the spaces on the first floor are sliding and can be recessed.

Architect: studio mk27 /
(Marcio Kogan and Diana
Rodomysler)
Location: São Paulo, Brazil
Photography: Pedro Kok

031

Swimming pools do not need to be square or have classical measurements. In this case, a long, narrow pool has been built in the space available along one side.

032

Wooden armchairs can be very uncomfortable. However, if they are wide and have armrests, soft cushions can be placed in them, which also gives you the option to modify the decor.

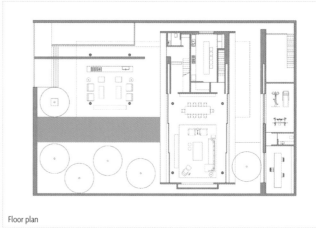

Floor plan

033

The rusticity of the stone wall stands out against the modernity of the rest of the house. Stone walls are solid and beautiful, and can provide a space with some coolness in the summer.

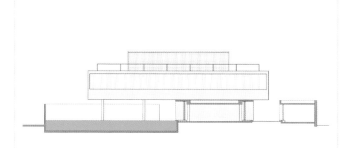

Elevation

034

This interior patio separates the main volume from the secondary one, which is a home office. A tree provides strength, volume, color, and presence without requiring great care.

Casa a Rayas

A young couple looking for a simple, easy to maintain, and functional home with three bedrooms commissioned this house, which consists of two separate volumes. The first is for the bedrooms and the second for living areas. The terrace is divided into three spaces: a pool, an exterior dining room with a grill, and an outdoor living room.

Architect: Estudio Martín Gómez Arquitectos
Location: Arenas de José Ignacio, Punta del Este, Uruguay
Photography: Ezequiel Escalante

035

This pool is stuccoed in gray cement. On one side, a stone wall features a great jet of water that is used to fill the pool.

036

The architects combined cedar wood with gray granite stone surfaces for the exterior of the house. They painted turquoise and white stripes on the wood in imitation of European beach awnings.

Architect: Martín Gómez Arquitectos (Martín Gómez and Gonzalo Veloso)
Location: La Boyita, Punta del Este, Uruguay
Photography: Ezequiel Escalante

This house consists of five separate volumes, one of which is used for the living areas and the rest for bedrooms. The pool is the center of the project, and the rest of the building revolves around it. The galleries between the blocks create an open living area and a fluid transition between the interior and the exterior.

037

A bed or couch with a canopy can be placed on a large terrace. It brings originality and grandeur to the space and is very flexible furniture for gatherings with family or friends.

038

In hot and rainy climates, it is a good idea to cover part of the terrace so that the outdoors and nature can be enjoyed even when the weather is poor.

Elwood House

Architecture: NMBW
Landscape design: Michael
Wright, Catherine Rush
Location: Melbourne, Australia
Photography: Michael Wright
and Peter Bennetts

The outdoor area of this house is a simple and practical yard where stone and wood take pride of place. In one corner is a small fireplace that calls to mind ones from years gone by. The space is austere, and there is little vegetation, which reduces care to a minimum. The fence is made of wood, just like the exterior walls of the house and the outside table.

039

You can buy structures for making fireplaces. This one is made of stone and has a storage space for combustible materials.

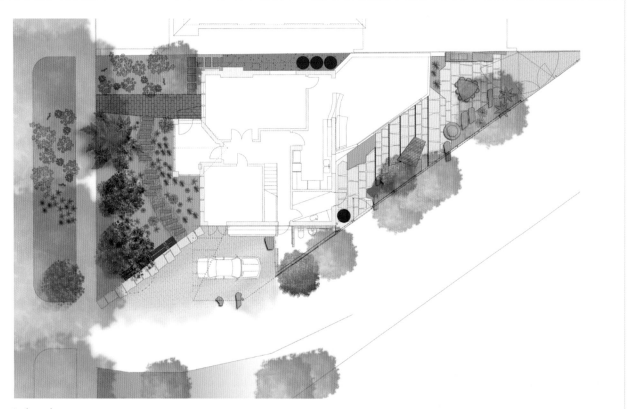

Landscape plan

040

A stone floor is easy to clean and maintain in good condition. The sparse furniture is varnished to protect the wood from the weather.

Summit Drive

This house is an extension to a steel and glass home built in the 1970s. The annex, which is a large terrace, was built with the intention of turning it into a relaxation and entertainment area. The terrace has simple geometric shapes and a low bare concrete wall that gives it a sense of austerity.

Architect: XTEN Architecture
(Scott Utterstrom)
Location: Beverly Hills, CA, USA
Photography: Art Gray

041

The arbor is set apart from the more conventional structures by its metal rods and the plates that cover it.

The couch's pure white lines contrast with the unpainted, unpolished, and unworked wall behind.

House in Estoril

The house was refurbished to achieve a more regular structure. The various volumes overlap and make up a monolithic construction enhanced by its materials. The house is divided into two clearly demarcated public and private spaces. The living area is dynamic, with entrances from the various gardens. Large windows in the relaxation area on the top floor make full use of the light.

Architect: Frederico Valsassina, Rita Silva, and Joana Quintanilha
Location: Estoril, Portugal
Photography: FG + SG Fotografia de Arquitectura

042

From a distance, the residence looks like a glass house due to its large windows. An almost bare backyard helps set off the simplicity of the shapes.

043

A climbing plant requires little care and naturally beautifies a wall. In this case, the plant strip connects with the rest of the site—a very green living area.

Majadahonda

This terrace consists of a set of two couches and a center table beneath a wooden arbor, the roof of which can be expanded or retracted because it is a white canopy that operates in the same way as a blind, only horizontally. The cushions and small decorative details bring a touch of color to the somewhat neutral set.

Landscape design: Alba Garrido for Greendesign
Location: Madrid, Spain
Photography: Nacho Uribesalazar

044

Playing with colors when decorating any space is simple and works well. Choosing one or two complementary shades and ensuring that small objects coordinate is a good option.

Mhouse

Architect: XTEN Architecture
(Monika Häfelfinger, SIA; and
Austin Kelly, AIA)
Location: Venice Beach,
CA, USA
Photography: Art Gray

This dwelling was designed as a residence for an artist so he could work at home. The house consists of two L-shaped blocks that intersect, one set aside for work and one for home use. The painter's studio required a high ceiling, plentiful natural light, and excellent ventilation. The corridors link the studio and the living area while surrounding the patio.

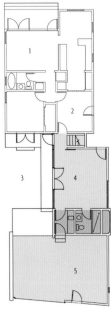

1. Living/gallery
2. Gallery
3. Courtyard
4. Video studio
5. Painting studio
6. Video wall
7. Open to below
8. Roof deck

Ground floor plan

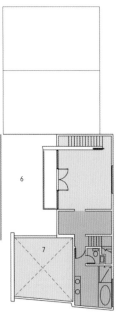

Second floor plan

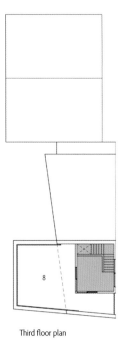

Third floor plan

045

The decoration of this space is minimalist and focuses on color. The doorframes, the table, stairs, and shelving are orange, and together provide a feeling of harmony.

046

Leaving a large wall in the garden or terrace and painting it white is the perfect excuse to install an "outdoor cinema."

Axial Symphony

The designers of this house sought to create a symmetrical space in which the inhabitants could achieve a state of experiential and spiritual balance. The starting point for this project is the manipulation of the central axis. The furniture in each room is laid out in the space in relation to the same axis so that the individual is always at the epicenter of the space.

Landscape design: Design Systems Ltd (Lam Wai Ming, Fanny Leung, Fang Huan Huan, Zhang Xing, and Lansy Dai)
Location: Shenzhen, China
Photography: Design Systems Ltd

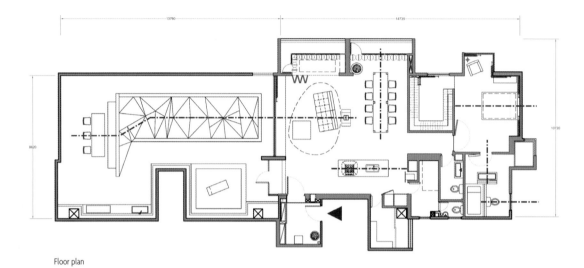

Floor plan

047

The original terrain in this terrace with volume was altered to create the green hills that coincide with the axis of the window and the living room couch. The effect is innovative and relaxes the eyes.

Prototype

Landscape design: Nicole
Helene Designs
Architect: Works Partnership
Architecture
Location: Portland, OR, USA
Photography: Shawn St. Peter

This small house has been remodeled in order to accommodate a young family with two children. Given the small size of the apartment, specific furniture was designed to fit in the various spaces and meet the needs of the inhabitants. The terrace is simple and practical but preserves a design that is in keeping with the rest of the house.

048

The sturdy wooden table will remain in good condition for quite a long while. The lamppost, in imitation of an old oil lamp, is a special detail.

049

The orange lights draw new shapes and, together with the dark wood, add warmth.

Soto Moraleja

The color range of this outdoor space is controlled down to the smallest detail. The white of the two center tables contrasts with the dark grey of the couches. The touch of color is provided by the cushions in two contrasting colors: green and beige. Green coordinates with the terrace's plants, while the beige is repeated in the flower of the center plant.

Landscape design: Tania Stefanova for Greendesign
Location: Madrid, Spain
Photography: Nacho Uribesalazar

Villanueva

This terrace is dominated by neutral tones in the relaxation area, with white furniture and the structure of a very dark aluminium arbor, which is coordinated with the ceramic tile flooring. The pool area, however, is full of contrasts. The green lawn is enhanced by the turquoise of the pool. As a whole, the space is practical, simple, and versatile.

Landscape design: Alba Garrido for Greendesign
Location: Madrid, Spain
Photography: Nacho Uribesalazar

050

The white awning does not create marked shadows, and it reduces the entry of direct light without forgoing brightness.

Casa C-24

This house is notable for the simplicity of its shape and structure. With geometric lines, Casa C-24 is divided into three volumes interconnected with the outside through large windows that open onto the first-floor garden. The kitchen and living room are separated by a 13 ft. (4 m) high sliding door, which creates a larger and brighter space.

Architect: Ábaton Arquitectura
Landscape design: Batavia
Location: Madrid, Spain
Photography: Belén Imaz

051

A large window will always give the feeling of more freedom, light, and space. Choose thick, good-quality glass to retain the room's heat and muffle street noise.

Second floor plan

Ground floor plan

Guijo

This family home is the result of the comprehensive remodeling of an old barn. The rooms are sited around the two large central areas: the living room and kitchen. Basic materials—water, iron, and cement—have been used along with the existing stone. The house has solar panels that provide energy in summer and two turbines that use the beds of two streams to supply electric power to the storage heaters in winter.

Architect: Ábaton Arquitectura, in partnership with Batavia
Location: Cáceres, Spain
Photography: Belén Imaz

052

This patio has a natural spring of water gushing from a rock, which cools the house in the hottest months.

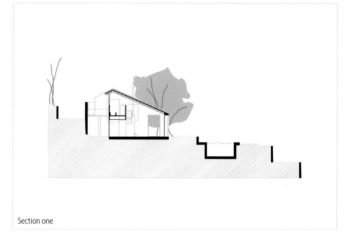

Section one

The natural pool is actually a reservoir through which water continuously flows and irrigates the pastures.

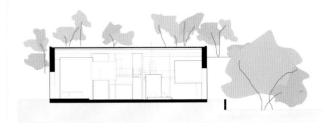

Section two

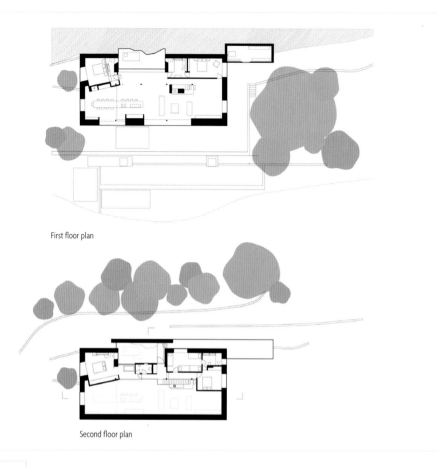

First floor plan

Second floor plan

053

The refurbishment plan respected the original appearance of the barn and its surroundings, so the house blends into the natural landscape and does not stand out above the vegetation.

The majority of freestanding houses in Holland are situated in the middle of a plot, leaving the sides empty. By contrast, this house uses the complete building plot, and its patio is on the inside. The entire house is arranged around this patio. The outdoor and indoor spaces alternate rhythmically. All the rooms have access to the patio, which functions like an ancient Roman cloister. The part that faces the street can be closed off using reinforced blinds.

Steel Study

Architect: Eric Vreedenburgh
(Archipelontwerpers)
Location: Leeuwarden,
The Netherlands
Photography: Marcel van
der Burg

054

A gray grille surrounds and provides privacy to the house, while the holes in the grille lessen the feeling that it is a rigid and impassable barrier.

The slope leads down to the garage
entrance, which is in the basement
underneath the house.

Second floor plan

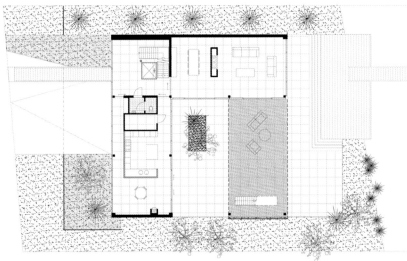

Ground floor plan

055

An upper terrace has been built in the inner patio to provide the upstairs bedrooms with outdoor space. Furthermore, the U-shaped structure affords marvelous views.

São Bento Residence

This residence is situated on a 49 ft. x 148 ft. (15 m x 56 m) lot. It was designed to provide maximum sunlight in the upper bedrooms by extending the lower floor and providing a terrace. The curve on the top floor is one of the most striking architectural features of this construction. Overhead lighting provides soft illumination, which makes it possible to close the house on its sides, thus providing more privacy.

Architect: Anastasia Arquitetos
Location: Belo Horizonte, Brazil
Photography: Jomar Bragança

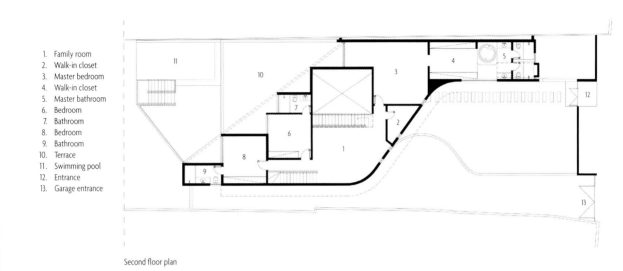

1. Family room
2. Walk-in closet
3. Master bedroom
4. Walk-in closet
5. Master bathroom
6. Bedroom
7. Bathroom
8. Bedroom
9. Bathroom
10. Terrace
11. Swimming pool
12. Entrance
13. Garage entrance

Second floor plan

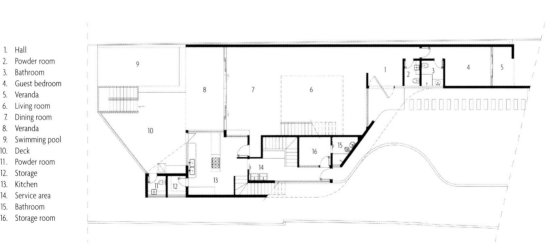

1. Hall
2. Powder room
3. Bathroom
4. Guest bedroom
5. Veranda
6. Living room
7. Dining room
8. Veranda
9. Swimming pool
10. Deck
11. Powder room
12. Storage
13. Kitchen
14. Service area
15. Bathroom
16. Storage room

First floor plan

056

A touch of green can bring life to any nook. Plants that do not require much care, such as cacti, are ideal for this type of space.

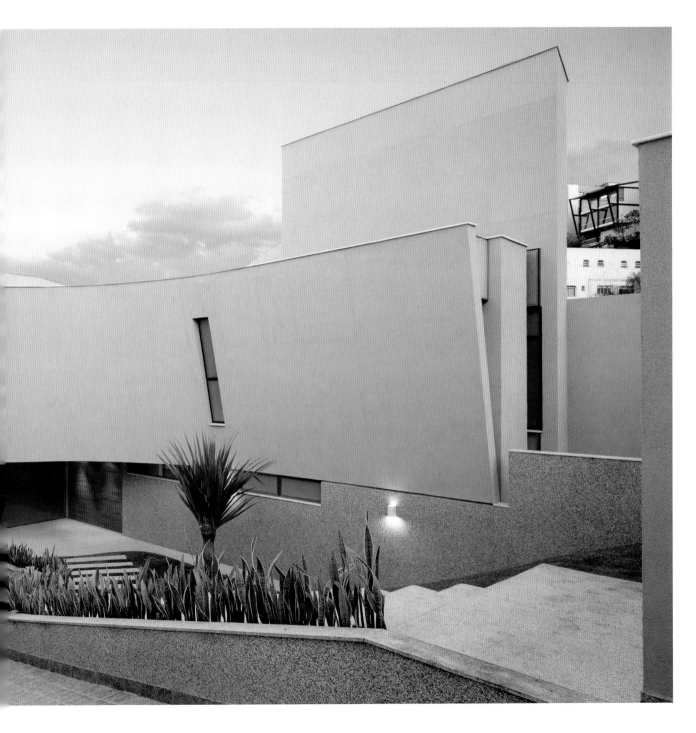

057

Stone floors are very hard, tough, and easy to clean. They take away warmth from a space but do provide a rustic look, which can be very attractive, depending on the ambience.

058

The terrace provides an outdoor space on the top floor, and also serves to shield a relaxation area near the pool.

Open Box House

This house results from the refurbishment of a run-of-the-mill box home. Interior walls were removed to create a large, open plan that centers the house on a new kitchen. Floor-to-ceiling windows were added to offer stunning views. Steel and aluminum finishes contribute to its clear and clean design.

Architect: Feldman Architecture
Location: San Francisco, CA, USA
Photography: Paul Dyer

059

Previous: The design and materials of the stone and wood bench match the house, and the red chairs lend a touch of color. At the end of the yard, the tall bushes beautify the space and provide privacy.

This Brazilian house stands on a mountainside and has just one large floor, which covers 4,305 sq. ft. (400 m²). It is a second home and was designed from an existing steel frame at the meeting point of indoor and outdoor spaces, evoking lightness, openness, and warmth. The house is L-shaped and goes around part of the garden and pool. The architectural structure mixes strong and hard-wearing materials with the ethereal consistency of the glass.

Architect: Luiz Eduardo Indio da Costa
Location: Pedro do Rio, Petrópolis, Brazil
Photography: Mario Grisolli

060

An arbor that changes the
extension of the roof is ideal for
creating indoor-outdoor spaces.
In this case, it is a mobile
platform.

061

It can be a good idea to lay wooden decking on terraces to prevent reflected sunlight bouncing up and bothering your eyes, especially when it is at its brightest.

062

If you live in an area without too much pollution, you can put a telescope on the terrace and enjoy a starry sky.

Casa Palillos E-3

This house stands on a sloping lot, which allows for three levels built with a variety of materials and textures that create intertwined outdoor and indoor spaces. The client wanted to have ocean views from common areas—which should always be considered the most important areas in the house. The social area is located on the second level and has access to an infinity pool that visually adjoins the sea.

Architect: Vértice Arquitectos
Location: Peru
Photography: Vértice Arquitectos

063

Tables with glass tops, which expose the structure of the furniture, are an unexpected element in an exterior space. They are ideal in hot climates where there is never any snow or hail.

Pacific Heights Town House

A plan for remodeling a Victorian house from the early twentieth century was devised for this residence. The clients wanted to maintain the building's traditional feel, but also to infuse some modern elements and make the house as green as possible. The backyard had to be accessible from a number of spaces, and living areas were placed on the top floor, where the light was best and where a roof garden was added.

Architect: Feldman Architecture
Location: San Francisco,
CA, USA
Photography: Paul Dyer,
Roland Bishop

064

Tiered flooring can be used to store garden tools, cleaning equipment, and toys underneath the stairs.

Bahia House

The building is laid out around a central patio to maximize natural ventilation and keep the interior cool in hot weather. The whole house is designed to ward off high temperatures and excessive sunlight, and to that end, the architects used traditional Brazilian techniques involving clay roofs and wooden ceilings. Bahian houses use the northeast wind blowing in from the sea to cool the entire house.

Architect: studio mk27 / (Mario Kogan and Suzana Glogowski)
Location: Salvador, Brazil
Photography: Nelson Kon

065

The small holes of the latticed wooden panels separate the spaces to let air but not light through and lessen the strength of the wind. They also provide privacy.

066

A rug is a good addition to any
space because it adds a risk-
free splash of color. These are
indoor rugs, but there are others
specially designed for terraces.

Dovecote Barn

This project is an extension to a barn that was converted into a house. The clients wanted to extend the rear of the house to create more space and add depth to the building. The extension becomes the new dining and informal social area, with direct access to the children's play area and to the garden. The architects retained the character of the original barn despite using innovative and high-quality materials.

Architect: Nicolas Tye Architects
Location: Great Amwell,
Hertfordshire, United Kingdom
Photography: Nerida Howard

067

Lavender is a plant that is easy
to care for and grows best
on dry and sunny land. It is
attractive, easily recognizable
by its color, and famous for its
medicinal properties.

068

The water features along the boundary that separates the patio from the garden are a modern and practical decorative item. The sound of water is relaxing.

House Lam

Architect: Nico van der Meulen
Location: Bedfordview,
South Africa
Photography: David Ross,
Barry Goldman, and
Nico van der Meulen

The clients asked for a refurbishment and extension of an old house built in the 1950s on steep terrain with views of 270°. An infinity pool was placed near the bluff to offset the height difference. The pool starts very close to the living room, so when the sliding doors giving onto the terrace are opened, there is the feeling that everything is in a single area. The house was expanded to accommodate two garages and three bedrooms.

069

This terrace provides plenty of ideas about how to illuminate an outdoor space. The ball-shaped lamps are minimalist and elegant, and the torches in the background are in an ethnic style.

070

The pool is so close to the living room that when you open the doors, you seem to be in it. This creates a sense of a unique, shared, and large space that is free of architectural barriers.

071

A natural stone staircase is always a fine addition to the exterior of a house, especially if the house is located in a wilderness-type environment.

Pretty Beach House

Pretty Beach House is an Australian guesthouse situated within a ninety-minute drive from Sydney. This sophisticated house is surrounded by angophoras and has views looking down to beautiful sparkling Brisbane Water. Located in such a magical setting, the place has a fantastic pool and comfortable facilities decorated with rustic furniture that gives the scenery a timeless character.

Architect: Bells at Killcare
Location: Pretty Beach, NSW
Bouddi Peninsula, Australia
Photography: Bells at Killcare

072

If you have an exterior table and want to add a tablecloth, choose the fabric wisely. Opt for waterproof materials that can withstand the rain. Plastic tablecloths in beautiful patterns or textures are a good choice.

Roof Gardens

City Rooftop

Landscape design: Secret
Gardens of Sydney
Location: Sydney, Australia
Photography: Jason Busch

This rooftop garden is on the top of a twenty-five-story building surrounded by other skyscrapers. Geometric shapes are essential to the design of this space, in which a circular area with grass dominates the scene. A table, chairs, and two benches, visually separated by wood, turn the front area into an eating or resting nook.

073

The wooden seats frame the roof and provide a seating area where the space and the views can be enjoyed.

074

The geometrically shaped bushes are a formal element, while the lavender and iris plants add a free and easy air.

City Penthouse

Spanning three levels, this city penthouse was in need of a makeover. The client wanted a low-maintenance rooftop garden to enjoy personally while also creating expansive entertaining spaces. Set against views of the harbor and city, the garden has ponds, walkways, an entire entertaining level, and a hot tub.

Landscape design: Secret Gardens of Sydney
Location: Sydney, Australia
Photography: Peter Brennan

Above, a small metal water feature decorates the platform leading to the next level. On the left, the hot tub overlooking the harbor is spectacular.

075

Some items, such as the water feature, stairs, and furniture, are made of wrought iron and painted black. They can be cleaned by simply rubbing gently with a damp cloth.

076

In this area, an artificial pond with plants was installed, which is vaguely reminiscent of a wetland and quite a surprise among so many urban features.

077

The marsh plants, such as *Acmella decumbens*, are ideal for beautifying the edges of the pond, concealing canvases or other artificial materials, and cleaning the water.

Marinka

This is a three-story penthouse apartment near the Dnieper River. The upper floor consists of a landscaped terrace covering 2,690 sq. ft. (250 m²). The house is decorated with detail and originality. Features include a cement bottle decorated with Braille writing, a stone pouf, and a red Maersk shipping container. The main element is a vertical garden that presides over and connects the various rooms.

Architect: 2B GROUP
(Vyacheslav Balbek, Olga Bogdanova, Alena Makagon)
Location: Kiev, Ukraine
Photography: Vyacheslav Balbek

078

The geometric illumination of this garden terrace brings a creative touch, and sun loungers on the wooden decking lend an air of relaxation. In winter, the glass pavilion is used.

The vine on the wall creates an interior
garden and gives a feeling of freshness.

079

This small shrub is anchored in a cement-covered pot and serves as a railing in front of the shaft that looks onto the inner courtyard.

STEREO
MCPS/BIEM
This compilation ℗ 1982 CBS Records
PROMOTION COPY ONLY. NOT FOR SALE.

1 ℗ 1980
Polar Music
Int. AB
Bocu Music Ltd.
2 ℗ 1981 CNR
Holland BV;
Northern
Songs Ltd.
3. ℗ 1980
Black Sheep
Music Ltd.

33⅓
RPM

1. LAY ALL YOUR LOVE ON ME–ABBA (B. Andersson/B. Ulvaeus)
2. STARS ON 45–DRIVE MY CAR (Lennon/McCartney)
3. ATTENTION TO ME–NOLANS (Findon/Myers/Puzey)
(from the CBS LP "BOP STROLL ROLL" CBS 85400)
CBS Records are the exclusive licensees for the UK
MADE IN ENGLAND
LYN 11763

MADE IN ENGLAND BY LYNTONE RECORDINGS LTD

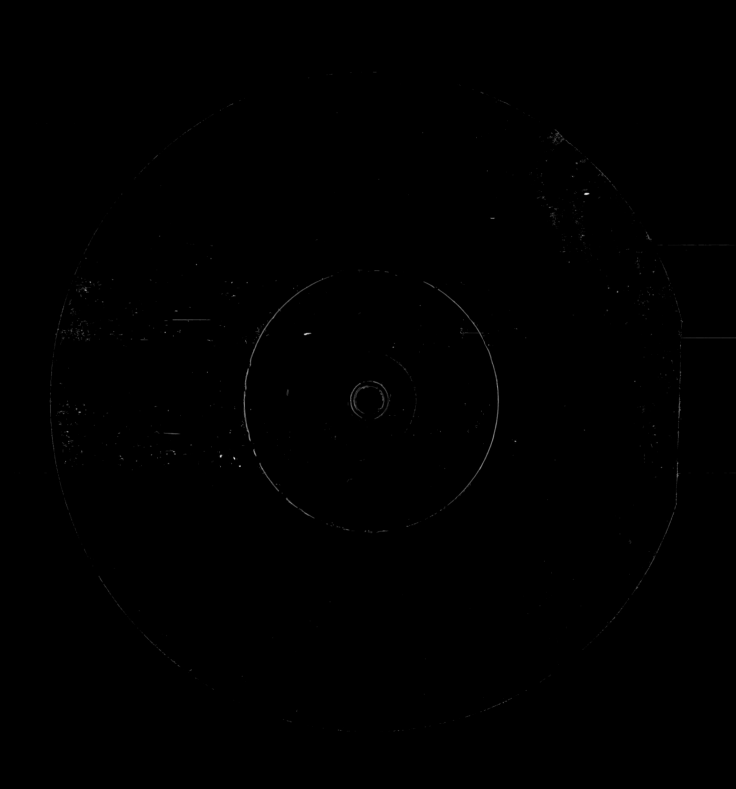

Regent's Park

Regent's Park has a terrace and a garden, both connected with the inside of the house through the repetition of shapes and materials. The seats repeat the form of the internal inglenook, while the interior and exterior spaces share the same wooden flooring. The outdoor spaces are minimalist and very geometric in style, and the plants complement their structures.

Architect: Amir Schlezinger
Location: London,
United Kingdom
Photography: Jerry Harpur

080

The bench follows the outline of the wall and is illuminated on the inside, thus providing orange light, which coordinates with the rest of the space in both form and color.

The terrace is divided into two areas by a row of sturdy cement pots containing plants.

081

The terrace is surrounded by plants and shrubs and is irregularly shaped. The sun lounger is positioned to compensate for the asymmetry of the two sides.

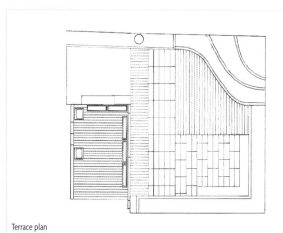

Terrace plan

Barrio Salamanca

Landscape design: Cristina
Garagorri for Greendesign
Location: Madrid, Spain
Photography: Nacho
Uribesalazar

Contrasts and oppositions predominate on this terrace. Divided into several zones by decorative awnings and spacers, this space is as practical and functional as it is elegant and well designed. The terrace contains a seating area, an area for eating, and a place with two sun loungers and no awning, for sunbathing.

082

A good way to separate spaces is by using large pots or planters. The result is optimal if you also add a small flower bed to mark the boundary of the areas.

Water Street House

This 2,370 sq. ft. (220 m²) house was built so as to become a historic piece in the future. Its 398 sq. ft. (37 m²) terrace provides fabulous views. The house fits in with the residential complex in terms of structure and appearance. The house has low-maintenance needs, and its materials are designed to age gracefully, adding interest to the construction.

Architect: Jason Fort
Location: St. Augustine, FL, USA
Photography: Jason Fort

083

It is increasingly common to find outdoor spaces with running water systems such as faucets installed. They are especially indispensable in outdoor kitchens.

084

The stools add a minimalist touch to the whole and are aligned with the wooden planks. The arbor frame is attached to the shed wall, and all elements are unified.

085

The pool was decorated with Zen motifs to reflect the proprietor's philosophy. These highly personal features bring originality to the space and reflect the personality of its owners.

SoHo Terrace

This roof garden is located atop a prewar apartment block in Manhattan, directly above a full-floor loft. The owners wanted a large terrace to accommodate several uses, including an area for children, another for dining and cooking, and a more private space adjacent to a home office and guest room.

Architect: Andrew Wilkinson;
Robert Glass
Location: New York, NY, USA
Photography: Garrett Rowland

086

A deck is the ideal space to install an outdoor sauna. The height of the terrace furnishes the space with privacy and quiet.

087

The kitchen, lounge, and dining space is best sited under an arbor to shelter it from rain or too much sun.

Almanzora

Almanzora is a set of apartments in two blocks, which are completely different despite being connected. The building facing the street is much simpler in comparison to other buildings in the area. The interior building has a circular structure with an open concrete façade that emerges from the basement and is broken down as it ascends.

Architect: Ábaton Arquitectura
Location: Madrid, Spain
Photography: Belén Imaz

088

Placing artificial turf on the roof helps insulate and preserve the inside temperature throughout the year, which saves up to 26 percent in energy costs.

089

The circular building has a
central courtyard providing
access to each apartment
through simply decorated and
easy-to-maintain open spaces.

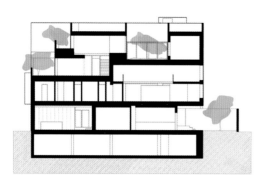

Section one

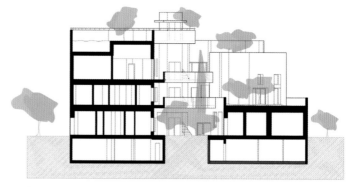

Section two

The circular building's roofs are all
landscaped, which allows residents to
enjoy silence and nature on top of an
apartment block.

Filadelfia Corporate Suites

The terrace of this hotel is a community space for customers, usually business travelers. The roof garden has 360° views of the city. The area is on the tenth and last floor of the building, which is 108 ft. (33 m) tall. A rectangular prism emerging from the center of the building presides over the center of the terrace and provides access to it, and also houses elevators and restrooms.

Architect: BNKR Arquitectura
Location: Mexico City, Mexico
Photography: Héctor Armando Herrera & Fabiola Menchelli

Basement plan

Ground floor plan

The rectangular prism ascends
throughout the building and ends
on the terrace.

090

The dark wood gives the space a contemporary and minimalist touch.

091

Aluminum furniture is used to decorate minimalist spaces because it visually lightens the space. It is practical because it does not rust and requires no special maintenance.

Casa en Las Dolomitas

This house is fenced by a 7 ft. 10 in. (2.4 m) tall wall made of horizontal wooden slats that bring out the perspective and cast shadows both from the sun and from the reflectors below. The house is surrounded by a deck made from 5½ in. (14 cm) wide ipê wood planks, which ends in a sunbathing platform fitted with a hot tub.

Architect: JM Architecture
Location: Campo Tures, Bolzano, Italy
Photography: Jacopo Mascheroni

092

The wooden decking can be covered completely with a white canopy that slides along rails placed on steel beams and thus becomes a retractable roof.

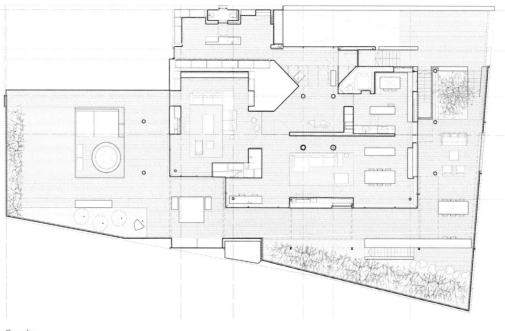

Floor plan

093

So that the home receives as
much light as possible, a custom
silicone structural enclosure wall
and huge sliding glass doors
have replaced the walls.

2 Bar House

The main goal in designing this home, in addition to convenience, beauty, and originality, was to keep construction costs to a minimum. Sliding doors on the first floor provide easy access to the patio. The roof garden allows the upper rooms to also have access to an outdoor space. Construction materials are low cost and ecological, in line with the clients' requirements.

Architect: Feldman Architecture
Location: Menlo Park, CA, USA
Photography: Joe Fletcher

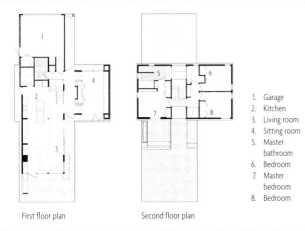

First floor plan

Second floor plan

1. Garage
2. Kitchen
3. Living room
4. Sitting room
5. Master bathroom
6. Bedroom
7. Master bedroom
8. Bedroom

094

Installing an electric fireplace in an outdoor space is a good way to have an exterior cooker in summer and a heat source in winter.

095

The roof garden in the picture is not intended for use as a relaxation area but rather is intended solely to beautify the house. Furniture could be added to turn it into a recreational space.

Ivy Street Roof Garden

This roof garden was designed during the renovation of an old warehouse into residential lofts. The terrace was planned off the penthouse space and built over an addition to the older building. To accommodate the weight and plants at the same time, three paving materials were combined: checker plate aluminum, plaster and concrete, and recycled lumber.

Landscape design: Andrea Cochran
Location: San Francisco, CA, USA
Photography: Andrea Cochran

096

The various volumes and shapes
of the planters give the terrace
a modern and original look.
The plants are easy to maintain,
which makes the terrace a
practical space.

Terrace sketch

097

The fence provides privacy
and is made of Plexiglas, which
allows the light to pass through
and changes the illumination of
the room throughout the day.

Greenwich Roof Garden

This private roof garden in Manhattan was built with lumber recycled from the water tank that had been on the roof. The wooden slats provide almost complete control of shapes and volumes, and this creates the illusion of waves or curves of the sun loungers. The edge of the roof is decorated with plants and is also a protective barrier.

Architect: Graftworks
Architecture + Design
Location: New York, NY, USA
Photography: David Joseph

098

The sun loungers were built on concrete and plaster platforms. Small storage areas were also built with wooden slats.

099

The wooden slats are raised at the edges of the roof in a curve to form waves that are reminiscent of the sea. The greenery emerges between the waves to add a touch of color.

Patios

This house is located in a residential and commercial zone five minutes from the train tracks. Since the surroundings were not aesthetically pleasing, it was decided to design the house so that it would look inward, reminiscent of ancient Roman houses. A large circular patio 49 ft. (15 m) in diameter arranges the structure of the house, and almost all the rooms face this atrium-like space. A terrace overlooking the patio crowns the building.

House Like a Museum

Architect: Edward Suzuki and
Toshiharu Nanba (Edward
Suzuki Associates)
Location: Kamakura City,
Kanagawa Prefecture, Japan
Photography: Edward Suzuki

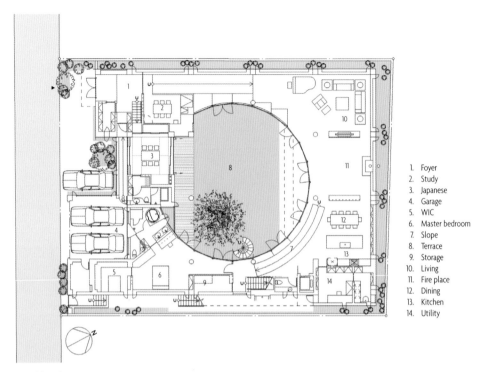

1. Foyer
2. Study
3. Japanese
4. Garage
5. WIC
6. Master bedroom
7. Slope
8. Terrace
9. Storage
10. Living
11. Fire place
12. Dining
13. Kitchen
14. Utility

Ground floor plan

100

The impressive circular patio presides over the house. The flower beds cover the roof of the rooms on the floor below.

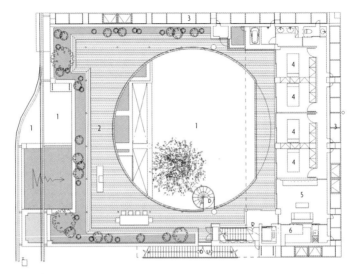

Second floor plan

1. Open
2. Terrace
3. Top light
4. Bedroom
5. Family room
6. Storage

The terrace is an outside space, but because it is interior, it is protected from street noise. The central tree, which rises to the top of the building, decorates the property, along with the plants in the flower beds.

101

The flooring and part of the furniture is made of bamboo. Bamboo wood is more environmentally friendly because the plant regenerates quickly.

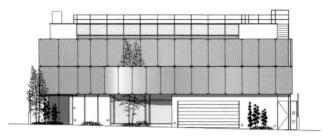

Elevation

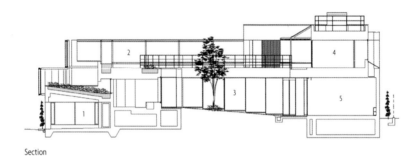

Section

1. Garage
2. Terrace
3. Terrace
4. Bedroom
5. Dining room

102

The glass of this terrace has moving parts for opening and closing to create breezes and ventilate the space, especially when the sun overly heats the room.

Annie Residence

The house was built for two families and is therefore split into two living areas: two pavilions connected by a glass hallway. The pool is the focal point of the project, and all the rooms in the house are laid out around it. Both pavilions have different levels, which creates pleasant spaces for enjoying the outdoors.

Architect: Bercy Chen Studio
Location: Austin, TX, USA
Photography: Mike Osborne

103

One way to create the effect of an interior patio without actually having one is for the building to go around part of the garden on three sides. If the walls are glass or have windows, the effect is enhanced.

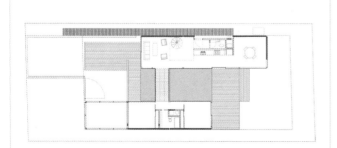

Floor plan

104

Ponds with plants should receive sunlight even if they are located in an interior patio. Plants require four to six hours of sun a day and must be protected against possible frost in cold areas.

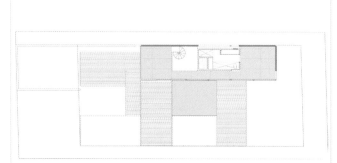

Floor plan

Cascading Creek House

This house was conceived as an outgrowth of the aquifers in the area. The house has two wings, one private and one public, and its roof is designed to collect rainwater for subsequent use. It is a smart house, controlled by an iPad, and it is self-sufficient for most of the year, thanks to its ecological heating system and solar panels.

Architect: Bercy Chen Studio
Location: Austin, TX, USA
Photography: Dan Bernstein,
Ryan Michael

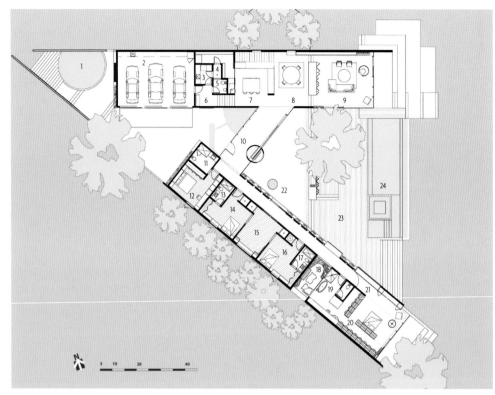

Floor plan

1. Entry pond
2. Garage
3. Laundry
4. Mechanical
5. WC
6. Mud room
7. Kitchen
8. Dining room
9. Living room
10. Entry
11. Guest bath
12. Guest bedroom
13. Bathroom
14. Bedroom
15. Playroom
16. Bedroom
17. Bathroom
18. Exterior courtyard
19. Master bathroom
20. Master closet
21. Master bedroom
22. Outdoor fireplace
23. Exterior courtyard
24. Pool

105

An inner courtyard with natural light is a perfect place for introducing natural exterior items into an interior. The gravel floor replaces a lawn and is easy to maintain.

106

The basin collects rainwater, which is then used to heat or cool the house via geothermal energy.

House with Three Gardens

Architect: Satoru Hirota
Architects (Satoru Hirota
and Yoshimi Kondo)
Location: Tokyo, Japan
Photography: Satoru Hirota
Architects

The special feature of this two-story Japanese house is the three patios spread around the dwelling. One is inside, another is outside, and the third is a terrace. The interior patio consists of a dry tree anchored in a small flower bed, surrounded by concrete. The combination of nature and construction material is what makes this space special.

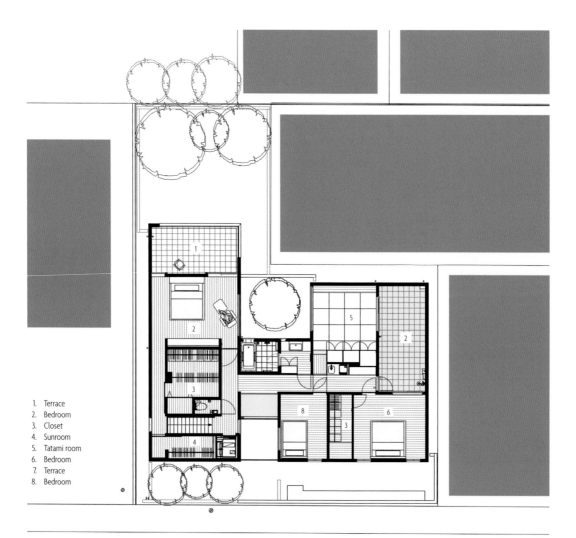

1. Terrace
2. Bedroom
3. Closet
4. Sunroom
5. Tatami room
6. Bedroom
7. Terrace
8. Bedroom

Floor plan

107

The interior patio can be seen from several areas within the house and reaches both floors. Its two glass walls and the concrete around it turn it into a sanitized space.

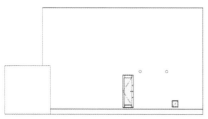

South elevation

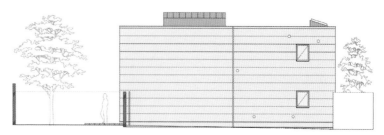

North elevation

East elevation

West elevation

The other two outdoor spaces round
off this curious residence. There are few
plants throughout the house.

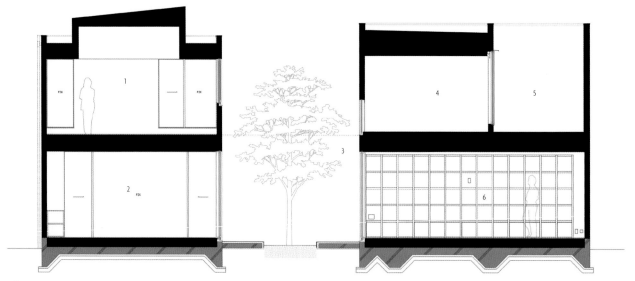

Section

1. Bedroom
2. Living room
3. Garden
4. Tatami room
5. Terrace
6. Study room

Balconies

Clarendon

This house, located at the top of Clarendon Heights, has views of the city in almost every direction. The home boasts plenty of natural light and has been furnished by its owner, interior designer Geoffrey De Sousa. Clarendon has two outdoor spaces, a terrace and a courtyard, which are thematically connected with each other thanks to De Sousa's decoration.

Architect: Mark English
Location: San Francisco, CA, USA
Photography: Matthew Millman and Cesar Rubio

108

The space is lit with two simple lanterns placed on the table. The orange and brown tones complement the warmth of the place.

109

Lanterns are used once more. The wood on the center table is distinctive and complements the gravel flooring. Together, they make the space seem more arid.

The architects decided to re-form the house by remodeling the interior, leaving the exterior intact so that it would fit in with the other houses around it. One of the things that set this house apart from the others that remain from the period is the layout of its spaces and the fact that the kitchen and dining room are near the entrance.

Architect: ONG & ONG
Location: Republic of Singapore
Photography: Tim Nolan

Ground floor plan

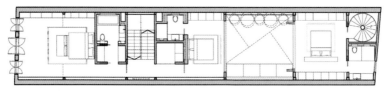

Second floor plan

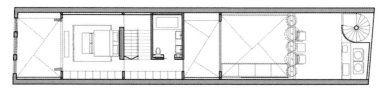

Attic floor plan

110

Since social gatherings often revolve around food, the architects decided that the kitchen and dining room should be next to each other so that guests and hosts can interact.

Bamboo is a recurring theme throughout the house, and this, combined with the neutral color of the walls, is ideal for rental housing in which different types of tenants may live.

Sky Garden House

This is a two-family residence in the city center. The building is designed to create two separate yet interconnected dwellings so that each family can enjoy their privacy but also interact freely. The interior of the house is presided over by a tree in an inner courtyard.

Architect: Keiji Ashizawa /
Mariko Irie
Location: Tokyo, Japan
Photography: Daici Ano

111

The small wooden-floored inner courtyard is surrounded by two glass walls so the tree can be seen from the bedroom and the living room.

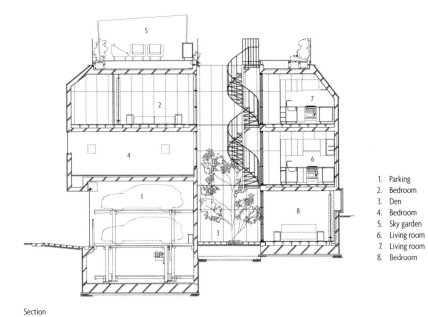

Section

1. Parking
2. Bedroom
3. Den
4. Bedroom
5. Sky garden
6. Living room
7. Living room
8. Bedroom

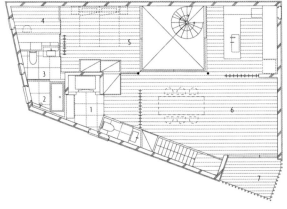

Third floor plan

1. Entrance
2. Bathroom
3. Lavatory
4. Den
5. Bedroom
6. Living room
7. Balcony

The spiral staircase connects the floors
through the courtyard.

Pacific Heights Victorian

This house was built in 1881 and has been refurbished. The clients asked for a tropical-inspired decor for the terrace. Given the small size of the space and its unusual L shape, an eating nook was designed. The cushions and parasol are customized. The fences coordinate with the rest of the house, and interior and exterior are intertwined.

Architect: Adeeni Design Group
Location: Pacific Heights,
San Francisco, CA, USA
Photography: Adeeni
Design Group

112

The green items, such as the ceramic table, help to highlight the plants. There are flowering plants that need little maintenance, such as geraniums, peonies, and aconites.

Architect: Ábaton Arquitectura
Interior design: Batavia
Location: Madrid, Spain
Photography: Belén Imaz

The terrace of this penthouse is designed to simulate a garden at ground level. All access areas were conceived as outdoor spaces and are decorated to give a sense of a single dwelling. The natural irrigation system uses rainwater descending from the roof to the terrace and from there to the lower terraces.

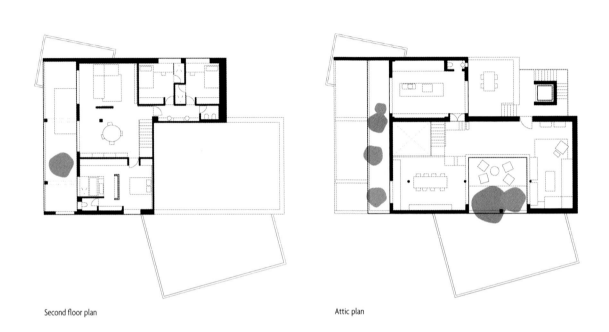

Second floor plan

Attic plan

113

The masses of moist soil mean the terraces are a thermal insulator.

Gramercy Town House

This three-story house in Manhattan retains its old façade, built in 1848, but is renovated inside, including its structure. The house, whose exterior walls are lined with red brick, has three bedrooms, three bathrooms, three terraces, and a roof garden. Inside, this Victorian-looking house is a work of art composed of steel, glass, and ceramics.

Architect: Fractal
Construction LLC
Location: New York, NY, USA
Photography: Eric Laignel,
Paul Warchol

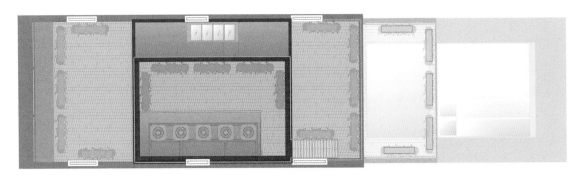

Roof deck plan

The impressive roof garden covers the
entire roof of the building and is divided
into two levels.

Casa CG

This house stands in the foothills of the Sierra Madre. Due to the slope of the plot, the architects had to adapt the design to the location. In return, the views are fantastic and the natural lighting enviable. The entrance is dominated by two oak trees that provide privacy and shade to the pool on the upper terrace. All rooms are fitted with large windows, and the flooring ranges in elevation by area to imitate the terrain.

Architect: GLR Arquitectos
Location: Monterrey,
Nuevo León, Mexico
Photography: Jorge Taboada

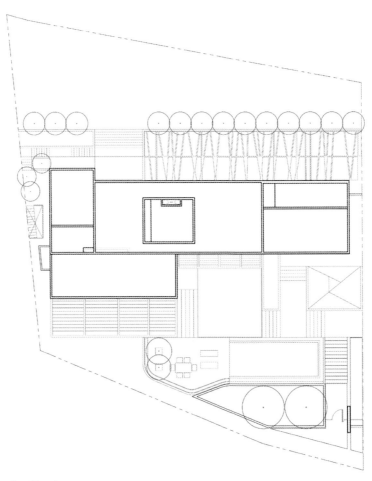

Ground floor plan

The house has two gardens and a terrace with a pool. The front garden is more formal, while the other, which is accessible only from inside the house, is more recreational.

114

The original wooden railing
fulfills its function, embellishes
the façade and also serves
as a planter.

This house was renovated with the addition of an L-shaped volume to the original construction, which modernizes the residence while preserving and embracing its core. Because the terrain is steep, the three stories cascade down toward the harbor, where a pool bonds the house to the sea. The large balconies and windows in the living area project the spaces toward the outside.

Architect: Luigi Rosselli, Edward Birch, and Pia Francesca
Location: Sydney, Australia
Photography: Justin Alexander

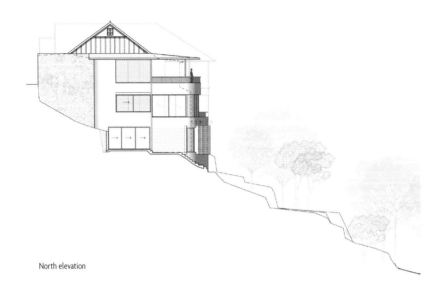

North elevation

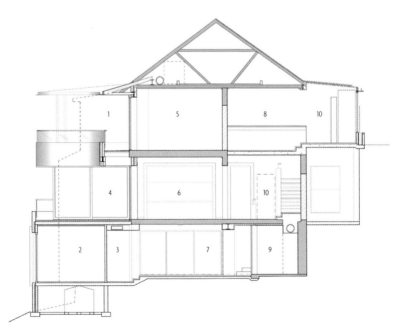

Section

1. Balcony
2. Bedroom
3. Hall
4. Terrace
5. Master bedroom
6. Living room
7. Rumpus room
8. Bridge
9. Cellar
10. Stairwell

115

Rounded shapes in neutral colors give a modern look to any construction. If you also add furniture with simple lines, the result is a very minimalist space.

Architect: Djuric Tardio
Architectes
Landscape design: Jeanne
Dubourdieu (Atelier de paysages)
Location: Antony, France
Photography: Clément Guillaume

This small, self-sufficient wooden French house was designed specifically for the family that was to live in it. This involved creating several exterior spaces so that the children could enjoy the outdoors and choosing modern, functional furniture that is ideal for a young person.

116

A wooden arbor creates shadowed areas. The effect would be even greater if creepers were planted to climb the structure, forming a kind of natural cabin.

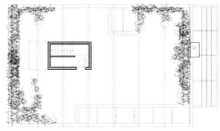

Terrace plan

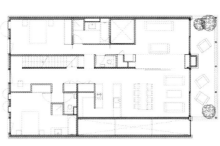

Second floor plan

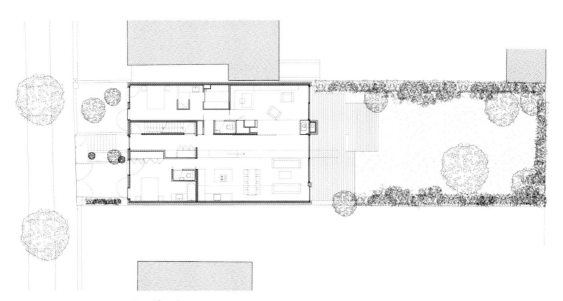

Ground floor plan

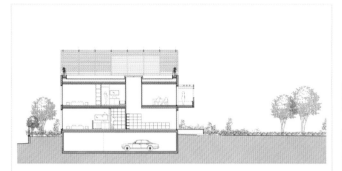

Longitudinal section

117

The entirely wooden frame of the arbor calls to mind buildings of the Old West, an effect that is reinforced with a swing made from the same material.

This house is inspired by nature and the flow of breezes. It represents them in a dynamic structure and an architectural design that employs various entrances and exits and external and internal spaces, intertwined in much the same way human beings sometimes join and sometimes move away from a crowd. Outdoor spaces are characterized by Japanese sobriety and minimalism.

Architect: Takashi Fujino /
Ikimono Architects
Location: Takasaki, Japan
Photography: Takashi Fujino /
Ikimono Architects

118

This simple, bare, and unpainted concrete balcony is decorated and furnished accordingly. If the idea was to create a little contrast, a few simple touches of color would completely change the space.

Nakahouse

This house is built on a hill, and the various levels between its different blocks imitate the curved shape of the site. The remodeling included opening up the exterior to the beautiful views, which had not previously been available, adding terraces to the bedroom wing, and building a large terrace to link the kitchen/dining area with the living room.

Architect: XTEN Architecture / (Monika Häfelfinger, SIA; and Austin Kelly, AIA)
Location: Hollywood Hills, CA, USA
Photography: Steve King

119

The sliding windows become doors and are concealed inside the wall, creating the feeling that they are not there. This roof garden is notable for its unexpected white color, in line with the rest of the house.

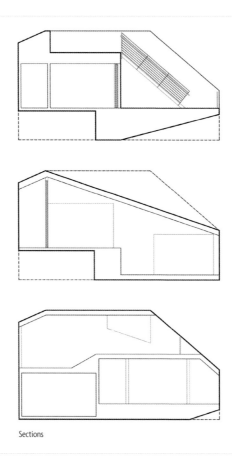

Sections

The exterior of the house is irregular
in appearance, while the interior is
geometric and almost aseptic. The white
walls and floor and the sliding doors
make the space seem unified.

120

The walls, made almost entirely from glass, allow you to see in from the outside if the lights are on. The decor is complemented by the façade in form and color.

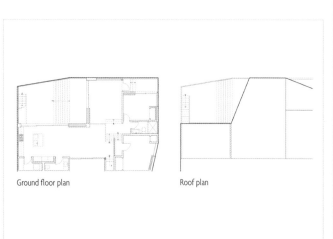

Ground floor plan   Roof plan

Vila Castela

Because of good local weather, this Brazilian house needs no heating and can be oriented toward the woods. This allows a greater sense of privacy for enjoying the beauty of the surroundings. The house is nearly 23 ft. (7 m) below the street and has three floors: a basement, a first floor with a pool, and an upper floor for the bedrooms. The house is constructed from concrete.

Architect: Anastasia Arquitectos
Location: Nova Lima, Minas Gerais, Brazil
Photography: Jomar Bragança

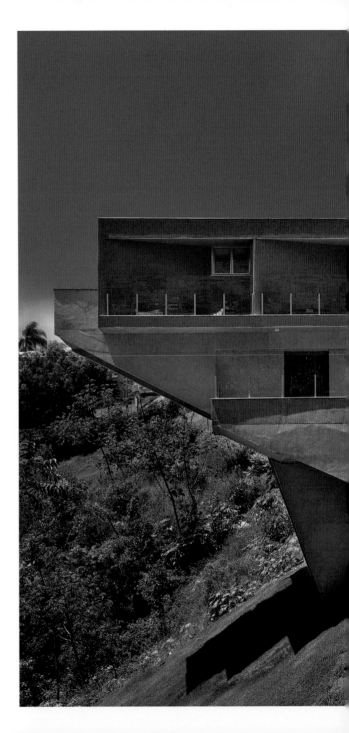

121

The house is painted terra-cotta, which makes it easier to maintain an unblemished façade given that the local gravel contains a pink powder.

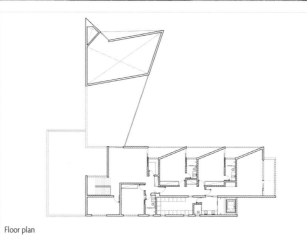

Floor plan

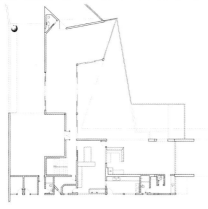

Floor plan

122

The relaxation area is entirely underneath the porch. The only uncovered part is the pool, wedged into the area closest to the drop; the pool thus contrasts with the green background.

Accessories

© UNOPIÙ

123

Make sure that wooden furniture does not get too wet, and protect it with plastic covers in winter to prevent water stains and the premature aging of the wood.

© UNOPIÙ

124

Wicker furniture lends a rustic air to an outdoor space. Its natural fiber and holes make it light and casual, and it is ideal for relaxing.

© KETTAL

©DEDON

125

Natural or synthetic? Today, many firms use very natural-looking synthetic fibers in their furniture that withstand the weather better and therefore last longer.

126

If you go for natural fibers, remember you have to clean them regularly to prevent dust from building up. Give them a coat of wax from time to time and put them in the shade.

© B&B ITALIA

127

Natural or artificial wickerwork is often used in classic furniture. It is increasingly found in innovative modern, original, and ergonomic products, too.

© B&B ITALIA

128

The seat and back of the chairs, which are made of rope, let air in through the structure and reduce the feeling of heat.

© KETTAL

129

The delicacy of the structure
of these sets is ideal for small
spaces because the furniture is
not visually bulky.

130

It is easy to add a touch of color to any space by taking advantage of the many furniture options available on the market. You can add accessories in similar shades.

131

The director's chair is an outdoor classic. Plus, because it can be folded, it can be stored almost anywhere.

132

Wrought iron is easy to shape, since it melts at more than 2,732°F (1,500°C) and cools and hardens quickly. This makes it especially useful for decorative items.

133

Rust can be removed from metal with sandpaper specifically designed for this material. If the furniture is painted, it is best to strip it before sanding with a specialized product.

134

Once the item is restored, protect it with antioxidant products such as red lead, which inhibits corrosion and helps set the product better. This primer can be sprayed on.

135

Wood or wicker furniture is easy to find and care for, and it ages attractively. Add good cushions to ensure that your couches are comfortable.

© DEDON

© UNOPIÙ

© UNOPIÙ

136

The best outdoor cushions are made of acrylic, polyester, or PVC. All these materials are water-and stain-resistant but are not protected from prolonged exposure to the sun.

© B&B ITALIA

© B&B ITALIA

137

Modernity also extends to outdoor furniture. Futuristic, ergonomic, and in vibrant colors, these chairs are sure to impress.

© B&B ITALIA

138

A couch with a canopy is decorative and private. It's like an outdoor bed but takes up less space, and it has a back, making it more comfortable for sitting.

© DEDON

139

If you are looking to surprise your guests, a large, round, and spectacular couch is ideal as long as you have enough space. These also tend to be very soft and comfortable.

140

A sun lounger is an essential item in outdoor spaces. Unlike chairs, tables, and armchairs, sun loungers encourage you to bask in the sun and relax to the full.

141

While perhaps not the most comfortable, wrought-iron sun loungers are aesthetically beautiful. If you have enough space, you can add a mattress lined with waterproof fabric.

142

Ergonomic sun loungers adjust to your body with ease, and although at first glance they may seem rigid, they are not. They fit seamlessly into terraces decorated with modern items.

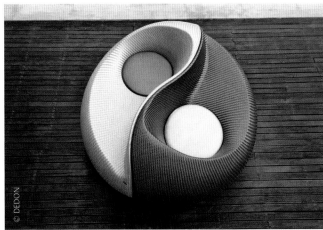

© UNOPIU

143

A large parasol in cream
shades with a wooden frame is
always elegant and beautifies a
space. In this case, the square
shape matches the form of
a table and leaves no corner
unshaded.

© GREENDESIGN

144

The frame and dome of this star-shaped parasol create different levels so it does not catch in the breeze, thus preventing warping or turning inside out.

145

The pole of a parasol can sometimes get in the way, so side-pole parasols and ones that hang from the ceiling have been developed that can also function as outdoor lamps.

146

Outdoor beds are ideal for hot climates and large outdoor areas because you can sleep comfortably under the stars and enjoy your terrace twenty-four hours a day.

147

The role of an arbor is to create shadows to provide protection from the sun. If tall buildings surround the outdoor space, an arbor can also help enhance privacy.

148

If you want to add a climbing plant, the best is ivy, which is also evergreen and provides shade in summer and lets in light in winter. Bougainvillea and jasmine will add color.

149

If you want to cover the arbor with a tarp, there are polyester and microperforated fabrics that are breathable, easy to clean, and can be gathered like blinds.

150

Drapes provide side protection, can create small, enclosed spaces outdoors, and can be drawn back by just tying them with ribbons to one of the posts.

DIRECTORY

2B Group
Kiev, Ukraine
www.2bua.com

Ábaton Arquitectura
Madrid, Spain
www.abaton.es

Adeeni Design Group
San Francisco, CA, USA
www.adeenidesigngroup.com

Amir Schlezinger
London, United Kingdom
www.mylandscapes.co.uk

Anastasia Arquitetos
Belo Horizonte, Brazil
www.anastasiaarquitetos.com.br

Andrea Cochran
San Francisco, CA, USA
www.acochran.com

Andrew Wilkinson
New York, NY, USA
www.wilkinsonarchitects.com

Archipelontwerpers
Den Haag, Netherlands
www.archipelontwerpers.nl

Bercy Chen Studio
Austin, TX, USA
www.bcarc.com

Bells at Killcare
Killcare Heights, NSW, Australia
www.bellsatkillcare.com.au

BNKR Arquitectura
Mexico City, Mexico
www.bunkerarquitectura.com

Design Systems Ltd.
Hong Kong, China
www.designsystems.com.hk

Djuric Tardio Architectes
Paris, France
www.djuric-tardio.com

Edward Suzuki Associates Inc.
Tokyo, Japan
www.edward.net

Feldman Architecture
San Francisco, CA, USA
www.feldmanarchitecture.com

Fractal Construction LLC
New York, NY, USA
www.fractal-construction.com

Frederico Valsassina
Lisbon, Portugal
www.fvarq.com

GLR Arquitectos
Nuevo León, Mexico
www.glrarquitectos.com

Graftworks LLC
New York, NY, USA
www.graftworks.net

Greendesign
Madrid, Spain
www.greendesign.es

Hierve Diseñería
Mexico City, Mexico
London, United Kingdom
www.hierve.com

Ikimono Architects
Takasaki, Japan
www.sites.google.com/site/
ikimonokenchiku

Indio Da Costa AUDT
Rio de Janeiro, Brazil
São Paulo, Brazil
www.indiodacosta.com

Jason Fort
Florida, USA
www.jasfort.carbonmade.com

JM Architects
London, United Kingdom
Manchester, United Kingdom
Glasgow, United Kingdom
www.jmarchitects.net

Keiji Ashizawa Design
Tokyo, Japan
www.keijidesign.com

Luigi Rosselli
Surry Hills, NSW, Australia
www.luigirosselli.com

Mareines + Patalano Arquitetura
Rio de Janeiro, Brazil
www.mareines-patalano.com.br

Mark English Architects
San Francisco, CA, USA
www.markenglisharchitects.com

Martín Gómez Arquitectos
Punta del Este, Uruguay
Buenos Aires, Argentina
www.martingomezarquitectos.com

Metropolis
Lima, Perú
www.metropolisperu.com

Molins Interiors
Barcelona, Spain
www.molinsinteriors.com

Nico van der Meulen
Johannesburg, South Africa
www.nicovdmeulen.com

Nicolas Tye Architects
Bedford, United Kingdom
London, United Kingdom
Peterborough, United Kingdom
www.nicolastyearchitects.com

Nicole Helene Designs
Vancouver, WA, USA
Portland, OR, USA
www.nicolehelenedesigns.com

ONG & ONG
Singapore
New York, NY, USA
www.ong-ong.com

Patrice Bideau
Auray, France
www.architectes.org/portfolios/a-typique/

Pitsou Kedem
Tel Aviv, Israel
www.pitsou.com

Roberto Silva Landscapes
London, United Kingdom
www.silvalandscapes.com

Rush/Wright Associates
Melbourne, Australia
www.rushwright.com

Satoru Hirota
Tokyo, Japan
www.hirotaa.net

Secret Gardens of Sydney
Sydney, Australia
www.secretgardens.com.au

Studio MK27
São Paulo, Brazil
www.marciokogan.com.br

Tim Davis Design
Ottawa, ON, Canada
www.timdavisdesign.com

Vértice Arquitectos
Lima, Perú
www.verticearquitectos.com

Víctor Cañas
San José, Costa Rica
www.victor.canas.co.cr

XTEN Architecture
Sissach, Switzerland
www.xtenarchitecture.com

ACCESSORIES

B&B ITALIA
Novedrate, Italy
www.bebitalia.it

GREENDESIGN
Madrid, Spain
www.greendesign.es

KETTAL
Barcelona, Spain
Coral Gables, FL, USA
www.kettal.es

UNOPIÙ
Soriano nel Cimino, Italy
www.unopiu.es